The Surname Chadbourne

Susan Morris &
Wendy Bosberry-Scott

ISBN: 1540742210
ISBN-13: 978-1540742216

The question of surnames, their origins, distribution and history, lies at the heart of genealogy as well as being fascinating in its own right.

In the 1980s and 1990s, long before many genealogical sources were even indexed, let alone online, our Surname Report service provided expert assessments of the origins, history and distribution of selected British surnames, using the sources available at the time.

Now, with so many more sources available, we believe that these reports retain their value as studies of individual surnames, and so we are gradually making the Debrett Surname Archive available online and in print for the first time. Some modern indexes have been consulted to refresh and update the reports.

Debrett Ancestry Research Ltd, PO Box 379,
Winchester SO23 9YQ
Tel: 01962 841904
Email: info@debrettancestry.co.uk
Website: www.debrettancestry.co.uk

CONTENTS

Overview

The use of surnames in England began in the Norman period, when surnames were not necessarily hereditary but usually a form of description. Some described the individual's trade or profession; others were nicknames; some gave the father's Christian name; others gave the individual's place of residence or origin.

Different surnames might be used in different documents, or more than one surname given in one document. Early descriptions were fairly elaborate and by the thirteenth and fourteenth centuries these were simpler, but still variable, and indeed the instability of surnames continued until well into the seventeenth century.

Although some Normans would already have had hereditary surnames on their arrival in Britain, the passing on of a surname from generation to generation only became customary in Britain gradually during the course of the thirteenth and fourteenth centuries. At the end of this period most of the population apparently had surnames.

Variations in the spelling of a family's surname continue to be found until the present century. Before this, as most people could not read or write, the parish clerk or other official would write down the name as they heard it.

There are four main groups of surnames:

A - Local names, which describe a person by his place of residence or origin.

B - Occupational names, which describe a person by his trade or profession.

C - Surnames of relationship, which refer to the Christian name of the father or other important relative.

D - Nicknames or sobriquets, coined to describe a person in terms of his appearance or character.

Many surnames have uncertain origins, but the name Chadbourne clearly falls into Category A.

Origins

The surname Chadbourne is included in P H Reaney's *Dictionary of British Surnames* (3rd edition, updated by R M Wilson, 1995) and in C W Bardsley's *Dictionary of English and Welsh Surnames* (1901). Reaney groups Chadbourne with several variants: Chaburn, Chadborn, Chadbon, Chadbone, Chadband and Chatburn; Bardsley lists as variants Chadband, Chadburn, Chadbourn and Chadbourne.

Both Reaney and Bardsley agree that the surname Chadbourne derives from the place-name Chatburn in Lancashire. We consulted Eilert Ekwall's *Oxford Dictionary of English Place-names*; this work draws upon a general survey of early and secondary sources including charters, deeds, the Domesday Book and maps, to chart the various early forms of a given place-name and thus explain its meaning. Ekwall includes Chatburn, which is Old English in origin and translates as *Ceatta's* stream. He cites an example of the personal name *Ceatta* from 983, appearing as *Ceattan mære* in the *Codex diplomaticus ævi Saxonici* (ed. J M Kemble, London 1839-48). He further states that during his work he found the place-name Chatburn in 1251 Charter Rolls and in 1258 in *Inquisitiones Post Mortem* as Chatteburn.

The personal name *Ceatta* has also given rise to other place-names such as Chatford, Chatley and Chatsworth.

Reaney lists the following early examples:

John de Chatteburn	1379	Yorkshire Poll Tax
William Chatburn	1449	Register of Freemen of the City of York

Bardsley noted two further entries in the Yorkshire Poll Tax Returns:

Richardus Chattburne	1379	Yorkshire Poll Tax
Henricus de Chatteburn	1379	Yorkshire Poll Tax

Thus a surname referring to Lancashire was found over the county border in Yorkshire by the end of the fourteenth century; it is possible that all these entries relate to a single family group. Neither Reaney nor Bardsley found any examples of the name in Lancashire.

Many surnames had found their way to London by the fifteenth century, but *A Calendar to the Feet of Fines for London and Middlesex 1189-1485* contains no references to the name Chadbourne *etc.* (The feet of fines was a means of conveying or settling freehold property, from the reign of Richard I up to 1834, when a Statute was passed to abolish the method and set up a simpler way of achieving matters.)

Distribution

C W Bardsley included a brief survey of the distribution of the names included in his dictionary (1901), using English and American directories. He noted a single occurrence of the name Chaband in a Boston directory of 1886. Chadburn did not appear in this directory, but there were 10 Chadbourns and 38 Chadbournes. He found no entries for the name Chadbourn or Chadbourne in an 1867 directory of Sheffield or of the West Riding of Yorkshire, but Chadburn appeared three times in Sheffield and three times in the West Riding directory.

The existing volumes of the English Surname Series (which is very incomplete) show no references to the name Chadbourne *etc*.

There were no entries for the name Chadbourne *etc* in H R Moulton's *Palaeography, Genealogy and Topography*, a sale catalogue printed in the 1930s listing historical documents, ancient charters, leases, court rolls etc.

In 1890 H B Guppy published his *Homes of Family Names in Great Britain*, still the only published work on surname distribution in Britain as a whole. His work was based on printed genealogies and a survey of county directories for the 1880s, in which he looked especially at the names of farmers, reasoning that they were among the most stable groups in society. Guppy restricted his study to names which appeared in a proportion of 7:10,000 or higher and he found no references to the surname Chadbourne *etc.*

George F Black in his study of *The Surnames of Scotland* (1948) found that the name Chadburn appeared in Aberdeen, probably as a recent introduction from England. He stated that the name probably came from Chadburn in Lancashire.

There are no references to the name in dictionaries concerned with Welsh or Irish names.

Many of the sources available for charting surname distribution through the centuries are necessarily confined to the wealthier sectors of the population: in general, nobody wanted to know the names of the poor but the names of those with money or land were naturally of interest to the authorities. However, one source that covers the whole of the social spectrum is provided by English parish registers, the earliest of which began in 1538 following a mandate that all parish priests should keep a weekly record of all baptisms, marriages and burials that took place in their parish.

An early survey of a cross section of parish registers for the years 1601 and 1602 was carried out in 1910 by F K and S Hitching; incidences of a particular surname are noted by parish and county, although with no indication of numbers of references. They noted the following appearances:

1601
Chadburne Winchcombe, Gloucestershire
Chatboune Padiham, Lancashire

1602

Chatborn   Lancaster
Chatborne   Lancaster
Chatburne   Padiham and Cockerham, Lancashire

The name had, by 1601, left the confines of Lancashire and Yorkshire and appeared in Gloucestershire as Chadburne. Cockerham and Lancaster are to the north west of Chatburn and Padiham is closer to the south east.

A useful guide to the distribution of surnames for the sixteenth, seventeenth and eighteenth centuries in England is provided by the indexes to wills proved, and administrations granted, at the Prerogative Court of (the Archbishop of) Canterbury, in London, which had superior jurisdiction over local ecclesiastical courts where wills were proved until 1858. The PCC thus provides a national index, although it is not a completely representative one, as testators whose wills were proved in the PCC were mostly among the wealthier members of society, and a disproportionate number of them were from London or Middlesex. A search of the online indexes to PCC wills (1583–1858) found the following entries for Chadbourne and its variants:

1608	James Chatborne, yeoman, Loughborowe, Leics
1612	Margery Chadburne/Chadborne, widow of St Ethelborough, London
1653	John Chadbuorne, yeoman of Leigh, Worcestershire
1653	Daniel Chatburne, gent, Steeple Cleydon, Buckinghamshire
1691	John Chatborne, bach, seaman, HMS Little Edward [of] London

1735	Thomas Chadborn, mariner of Ship Harrison of Norfolk
1738	Robert Chadburn, gentleman of St George Bloomsbury, Middlesex
1752	Elizabeth Chadbourne, spinster of St George Hanover Sq, Middlesex
1752	Jane Chadbourne, widow of St George Hanover Sq, Middlesex
1816	William Chadband, victualler of Bunhill Row, St Luke, Middx
1824	Richard Walker Chatburn, auctioneer of St Andrew Holborn, Middx
1839	Margaret Chadburn, spinster of Rugeley, Staffordshire
1839	John Chadborn of Gloucester
1844	Henry Chadband, hat manufacturer of Shipston upon Stour, Worcs
1852	Benjamin Chadband, hat manufacturer of Chipping Norton, Oxon
1854	Ann Chadband, widow of Tonbridge Wells, Kent

Most of these examples are from London, with the name found as Chadburne in 1612, Chatborne in 1691 and Chadbourne in 1752. In 1608 the name appears as Chatborne in Loughborough, Leicestershire, in the heart of England. It appears as Chadburne in Worcestershire in 1653. In the nineteenth century, the name Chadband appears in Oxfordshire and Worcestershire (as both men were hat manufacturers it is possible that they might have been related) and Tunbridge Wells in Kent. Finally, the name was found as Chatburne in Buckinghamshire in 1653. Thus by the seventeenth century the name Chadbourne *etc* was found in southern counties, far from its origins in Lancashire.

For the nineteenth century, H B Guppy's survey has been mentioned above. Another important Victorian source is the *Return of Owners of Land* of 1873, sometimes known as the Modern Domesday Book. This source lists, county by county, every owner of an acre of land or more, with their residence (not necessarily the address of their property) and the acreage of their holding. A handful of Chatburn (*etc*) entries appears in this survey:

Return of Owners of Land

Derbyshire	1	Chadburn
	1	Chatburn
Gloucestershire	1	Chadborn
Lancashire	2	Chatburn
Yorkshire West	1	Chadburn
	1	Chatburn

Chadburn was found in Derbyshire and the West Riding of Yorkshire. Chatburn had the highest showing with one appearance in Derbyshire, two in Lancashire and one in Yorkshire West Riding. The only other variant of the name found in the returns was Chadborn, in Gloucestershire.

The first decennial census return in England, Scotland and Wales was taken in 1801, but personal information was only recorded from 1841 onwards. From 1851, the age, occupation and birthplace is given for each member of the household, and so these records provide invaluable genealogical information. The latest return currently open to public inspection is that of 1911 and there are now national indexes to the returns from 1841 onwards, although these indexes are not wholly reliable. We found the following numbers for Chadbourne and its variants:

6 June 1841

Chadbourne (60); Chadbourn (45); Chaburn (2); Chadburn (295); Chatburn (187); Chadborn (67); Chadbon (13); Chadbone (13); Chadband (46)

30 March 1851

Chadbourne (41); Chadbourn (32); Chaburn (1); Chadburn (292); Chatburn (225); Chadborn (31); Chadbon (23); Chadband (20)

7 April 1861

Chadbourne (61); Chadbourn (28); Chaburn (5); Chadburn (338); Chatburn (275); Chadborn (49); Chadbon (20); Chadbone (22); Chadband (61)

2 April 1871

Chadbourne (163); Chadbourn (8); Chaburn (14); Chadburn (357); Chatburn (326); Chadborn (39); Chadbon (19); Chadbone (35); Chadband (87)

3 April 1881

Chadbourne (124); Chadbourn (69); Chaburn (1); Chadburn (418); Chatburn (371); Chadborn (56); Chadbon (36); Chadbone (41); Chadband (85)

5 April 1891

Chadbourne (170); Chadbourn (25); Chadburn (497); Chatburn (391); Chadborn (37); Chadbon (21); Chadbone (31); Chadband (101)

31 March 1901

Chadbourne (194); Chadbourn (35); Chaburn (3); Chadburn (519); Chatburn (453); Chadborn (57); Chadbon (41); Chadbone (41); Chadband (93)

2 April 1911
Chadbourne (258); Chadbourn (43); Chaburn (2); Chadburn (547); Chatburn (473); Chadborn (49); Chadbon (44); Chadbone (69); Chadband (160)

Most of the entries for the form Chadbourne found in census returns were from England with only two examples of the name found in the 1901 census for Scotland. Chaburn appeared in Scotland in 1871 with eight entries for the name and in Wales in 1911 with only one entry. Chadburn occurred in single numbers only in Wales and Scotland in 1911, 1901, 1881 and 1861. Chatburn occurred in Wales in 1871 with one entry; it appeared in Scotland for all the census entries (apart from 1911) but never reached double figures. Chadborn appeared in Scotland in 1901 with only four entries and Wales in 1911 with only two entries. There was one entry for Chadbone in the 1901 census. Chadband appeared in Scotland in 1891 with only three entries.

Printed Genealogies and Heraldry

Burke's *General Armory* (1884) lists a single coat of arms:

> **Chadborn** (of Barton House, Gloucester) Argent a griffin segreant.
> Crest - a demi griffin.

This may refer to the Gloucestershire Chadborn landowner found in the *Return of the Owners of Land* (see above).

The following references have been found to printed genealogies for families of the name Chadbourne, Chadborn, Chatburn:

> **Chadbourne**
> *Burke's Distinguished Families of the USA*
> *New England Register* xiii 339

> **Chadborn**
> *The Pedigree Register* (1907-16) i 228

> **Chatburn**
> *Genealogist's Magazine* (1969) 3
> R C Chatburn, *Carpe Diem* (1968)

Summary

To conclude, the name Chadbourne derives from the Lancashire place-name Chatburn. The place-name is Old English in origin and derives from a personal name, *Ceatta*, and the word for stream. Several variants were found for this name including Chadband, Chadburn, Chadbourn, Chadborn, Chadbon, Chadbone and the original name, Chatburn.

Throughout our research we have found that the name tended to remain in the northern counties of England, but did eventually travel south, appearing in London by the beginning of the seventeenth century. The name and its variants appeared in Scotland, Wales and Ireland in very low numbers in the census indexes we consulted. However, in the sources we have consulted, we have found no evidence of the name appearing any further south than London, nor have we found examples in the south west or south east.

Sources Consulted

P H Reaney, *The Origins of English Surnames* (London: Routledge & Kegan Paul, 1967)

P H Reaney & R M Wilson, *A Dictionary of British Surnames* (Oxford: Oxford University Press, 3rd edition, 1995)

P H Reaney, *Dictionary of British Surnames* (London: Routledge & Kegan Paul, 2nd edition, 1976)

P Hanks & F Hodges, *A Dictionary of Surnames* (Oxford University Press, 1988)

M A Lower, *Patronymica Brittanica* (London, 1860)

C W Bardsley, *Dictionary of English and Welsh Surnames* (1901: reprinted, Baltimore: Genealogical Publishing Co, 1967)

C L'Estrange Ewen, *Guide to the Origin of British Surnames* (London: John Gifford, 1938)

H B Guppy, *Homes of Family Names in Great Britain* (London, 1890)

Ernest Weekley, *The Romance of Names* (London: John Murray, 2nd edition, 1917)

Ernest Weekley, *Surnames* (London: John Murray, 1917)

George F Black, *The Surnames of Scotland* (New York Public Library, 1946)

Edward McLysaght, *The Surnames of Ireland* (Dublin: Irish University Press, 1977)

T J & Prys Morgan, *Welsh Surnames* (Cardiff: University of Wales Press, 1985)

F K & S Hitching, *References to English Surnames in 1601* (Walton on Thames: Bernau, 1910)

F K & S Hitching, *References to English Surnames in 1602* (Walton on Thames: Bernau, 1911)

Debrett's People of Today (Debrett's Peerage Limited: London, 1996)

The Oxford Dictionary of National Biography (online, 2004–2014)

The Concise Dictionary of National Biography, Part II, 1901–1950, (Oxford, 1961)

Burke's Family Index (London: Burke's Peerage Limited, 1976)

H R Moulton, *Palaeography, Genealogy & Topography* (Sale Catalogue, 1930)

Index to Prerogative Court of Canterbury Wills (The National Archives: online)

G W Marshall, *The Genealogist's Guide* (1903; reprinted, Baltimore: GPC 1973)

J B Whitmore, *A Genealogical Guide* (London, 1953)

Charles Bridge, *An Index to Pedigrees* (London, 1867)

Geoffrey B Barrow, *The Genealogist's Guide* (London: Research Publishing Co, 1977)

Sir Bernard Burke, *The General Armory* (London, 1884)

C R Humphrey-Smith, editor, *Burke's General Armory Volume II,* (Tabard Press, 1973)

The Return of Owners of Land (1873)

Eilert Ekwall, *The Concise Oxford Dictionary of English Place-names* (Oxford: Clarendon Press, 4th edition, 1960)

E G Withycombe, *The Oxford Dictionary of English Christian Names* (Oxford: Clarendon Press, 2nd edition, 1950)

W J Hardy & W Page, *A Calendar to the Feet of Fines for London and Middlesex: Vol 1 Richard I – Richard III (1189–1485)* (London, 1892)

Richard McKinley, *The Surnames of Oxfordshire* (English Surnames Series III: Leopard's Head Press, 1977)

Richard McKinley, *The Surnames of Sussex* (English Surnames Series V: Leopard's Head Press, 1988)

Richard McKinley, *The Surnames of Lancashire* (English Surnames Series IV: Leopard's Head Press, 1981)

Richard McKinley, *Norfolk and Suffolk Surnames in the Middle Ages* (English Surnames Series II: Phillimore, 1975)

George Redmonds, *Yorkshire West Riding* (English Surnames Series I: Phillimore, 1973)

The Norman People (London, 1874)

Debrett's Heraldry (London, 1933)

J P Brooke-Little, revised, *Boutell's Heraldry* (Frederick Warne: London, 1970)

Indexes to 1841–1911 Census Returns of England and Wales (The National Archives/*Ancestry*)

ScotlandsPeople: Indexes to Old Parish Registers, Testaments, Statutory Registers

www.ingramcontent.com/pod-product-compliance
Lightning Source LLC
Chambersburg PA
CBHW070255290526
45789CB00004B/1856